THAT TOOL
CALLED MONEY

YOUR GUIDE TO DISCOVERING
THE LIFESTYLE YOU CRAVE AND
HOW TO BUILD IT

Tiana B. Clewis

This publication is intended for educational purposes and does not take the place of legal advice from an attorney or investment advice from a licensed investment professional. Every effort has been made to ensure that the content provided in this publication is accurate and helpful for our readers at publishing time. However, this is not an exhaustive treatment of the subjects. If financial advice or other expert assistance is required, the services of a competent professional should be sought.

First Printing, 2017

ISBN: 1974282260
ISBN-13: 978-1974282265

Selah Financial Coaching
Midlothian, TX 76065

tiana@selahfc.com
www.SelahFC.com

Printed in the United States of America

DEDICATION

I dedicate this book to my two sources of endless love and inspiration, my husband, Boyd, and my "twin," Gabriel.

TABLE OF CONTENTS

INTRODUCTION

When my husband and I married, we were the typical blended American family. We had three kids with one on the way, no savings and at least two of what felt like every kind of debt there was. We also had two drastically different styles of managing money with no real understanding of the right way to do it.

At the time, we were both longing to build a better lifestyle and a part of me was struggling with the desire to step away from my steady paycheck to discover what my purpose was on this earth. Sadly, with this seemingly impossible mountain of debt looming over our heads, there was no way to make that happen.

We were stuck.

But we didn't stay that way.

What if I told you that there was a way to dig yourself out of the financial hole that you've created and transform your life into something that you only dreamed was possible?

Well, it's true. We did it and as you read through these pages, I'm going to show you the strategies that we used to make this transformation happen. You see, we didn't do anything magical or insane. We didn't come into a big inheritance or sell everything we owned to make progress. We didn't live on only rice and beans, drive cars that needed to be impounded or work hours so long our kids barely saw us. We simply followed a step by step plan that walked us out of our financial hell and into our dream lifestyle.

Now, before we get started, I want you to raise your right hand and repeat after me:

"I commit to financial success today!"

I know that this seems rather silly; after all, you're reading a book, not standing before a judge! But that commitment that you just made, it's important. It's important to you. It's important to your family. And it's important to the generations to come.

Let me be real with you. Sometimes this journey will be hard. Sometime you'll feel as if the universe is against you and you can never win. There will even be times when all you want to do is quit.

But if you can commit to achieving financial success, you will overcome the swirling feelings that come with this journey. Once you overcome those feelings, you will get to experience the peace, the joy, the excitement, the security and even the relief that comes after.

The pages of this book are filled with wisdom and they are filled with hope. The chapters in this book will save your financials and maybe even your marriage, your sense of self-worth and or your sanity. The words in this book have the power to transform your life, but you have to commit, truly and honestly commit, to the journey for that transformation to manifest.

I know that you can do it. I have absolutely no doubt. But at this moment in time, YOU have to decide whether or not you can.

Are you ready to commit to financial success?

Great! Let's get started.

CHAPTER 1 - LAYING THE FOUNDATION

Have you ever watched a building being constructed from start to finish? There are certain things that have to be done before they can really start putting the house together. The builders have to lay a foundation of various parts such as steel, plumbing and concrete. If they fail to lay the foundation correctly, the building is going to crumble long before it was supposed to.

When it comes to using that tool called money, there are four very important foundational elements that you will need to understand and embrace. Just like that building, if you fail to create the proper foundation in your financial life, the dream life that you worked so hard to build will come tumbling down, if you ever manage to get there at all.

SPEND LESS THAN YOU MAKE

The first thing is to understand the primary key to financial success: Spend less than you make.

Yes, I know that you know this. You are a smart person and you know that if you make $1,000 and only spend $900, you have $100 to save or invest. When you save $100 every pay period over and over again, or you place $100 in wise investments every pay period over and over again, you will begin to grow wealth. Build enough wealth and you can easily drop some cash on family vacations, newer cars, houses, business ventures and charitable organizations. Basically, spending less than you make allows you to create the lifestyle that you want without worrying about the next round of bills in your mailbox.

People certainly understand this concept, but for a lot of us, putting that knowledge to good use has not been going very well. In fact, you probably fall into one of these three common scenarios:

1. **Your income barely covers living expenses.**

   It is nearly impossible to spend less than you make when you need every penny to keep a roof over your head and food in your belly. You have probably cut most of your expenses to their bare minimum already, so there is nothing left to cut to even find money for saving or investing.

2. **Debt eats up your income before it hits your bank account.**

   Maybe you racked up credit card debt because life hit you hard and you did not have enough money to survive. Perhaps there is a shopping, gambling or other expensive addiction that ate up your cash, so you paid for necessities on the credit card. It could be that you decided you deserved that new furniture, those name brand purses or that guys' trip to Progresso, even though you did not quite have the money for it. Maybe student loan debt is killing you. Either way, your debt payments are so high, it consumes your paycheck, leaving nothing behind for building wealth.

3. **You spend every extra dime that you have.**

   You make enough money to cover living expenses and pay what debts you have, leaving "extra money" in your bank account. This extra money excites you because it is a well-deserved treat that you cannot help yourself but to spend. Whether it is on a trip, new clothes, or fancy nights out with friends, that extra money always finds its way into someone else's pockets instead of your own.

Does at least one of those scenarios have you nodding your head thinking, "Yep, that's me"? For my husband and me, it was the second scenario. We had what felt like two of every kind of debt before we got our financial act together and took our net worth from super negative to positive. A huge part of that was discovering how to stop spending every dime that we had so that we could transform our lives.

No matter which scenario matches your life, we have a plan to make that a thing of the past, but the plan will never work if you fail to embrace a "spend less than you make" mindset.

LEARN TO BUDGET

Ok good people, let's talk about the dreaded B-word: budget.

For many people, including my own husband a few years ago, the word budget was like the death toll for anything fun, interesting or simply worth doing. For some, budget conjures traumatic childhood memories of your parents denying you candy, new toys and Disneyland because it simply wasn't in the budget. It was like a club that was used to beat you over the head any time you dared to want to do something fun.

For others, it was a word that signified that you were broke, poor, or simply did not have the money to enjoy some basic luxuries in life. Needing to budget implied that you had "lack" and lack simply does not fit into the life that you envision for yourself. In fact, lack may even represent failure in your eyes.

Simply speaking, the word budget is a terrible word for so many people. Well, it's time for me to set the record straight.

A budget is a written plan for your money.

That's it! It's not a strait jacket or a fun killer. It is simply a written plan that tells your money how it is going to be used in that month. If you want to spend $1,000 to take a trip to Jamaica, put it in the budget. If you want to save $400 a month for a really nice car, put it in the budget. A budget is simply your plan for how you are going to spend your money that month.

Your budget is going to be one of the most important tools in your dream-building arsenal.

It Reveals Your Cash Flow

Have you ever looked at your paycheck and wondered where the heck all of your money went? The truth is that it's nearly impossible to spend less than you make without having a real picture of what you are actually spending. There is something about the human brain that always seems to underestimate how much money has been spent, so your estimate of $300 spent eating out each month is probably closer to $450 or $500.

You Can Plan Your Next Move, Realistically

When you don't know your cash flow, you can't figure out how much money you really have to work with to hit your goals. If you're only looking at your bills, you may think you have $600 to save for that new car, but when you add in all of the expenses that don't come with a bill, that may go down to just $150. If you had a budget based on your actual life, you would have identified that $150 early on and would have had time to decide on which expenses to cut out in order to turn that $150 into more.

You Can Adapt to Unexpected Changes
For a lot of families, an unexpected emergency or unplanned expense comes with the same question: What am I going to do now? When you have a budget, you can usually figure that part out pretty quickly. Sometimes, a school trip that no one knew to budget for means you cut your clothes budget for the month or pick up an extra shift. Your budget allows you to see what you have available to use and what quick adjustments to make so that the expense does not become a crisis.

It Creates Clearer Boundaries and Better Communication
This benefit is really for the couples. When you both have sat down and agreed upon the budget for the month, you are learning the art of compromise and communication. You are also establishing clear boundaries that both of you must work within, which actually enhances the trust in the relationship. Think about the number of money fights that you would avoid if you could indulge in your favorite hobby without issue because it was already agreed on in the family budget.

Now let me be clear, a budget includes every single purchase that you will make with your money. We believe in the zero-based budget and this budget literally takes every penny that you are going to make that month and applies it to an expense or savings category. What that means is a budget is not just a list of bills.

I cannot tell you how many times I have met with a new client and asked for a copy of their most recent budget, only to receive a list of their bills. That list would have their rent, the electricity and water, car notes, student loans, phone bill, credit

7

cards – you know, all of the expenses that you receive a monthly bill in the mail for. To them, that was the budget. In their mind, this list of bills qualified as an accurate representation of their spending.

It took some time before I understood that this belief came from poor budgeting practices that had been passed down from parent to child generation after generation. In fact, I had a mother with a young adult son tell me that she knew she had taught her son wrong about money management. One day she watched in horror as he made a list of his bills to see if his paycheck would last until the next payday and was satisfied when it did. What she had to point out to him afterwards, as I do with many of my clients, are the other expenses like food, gas and toiletries where you never receive a bill but still have to pay for somehow.

You see, that written plan for your money is not limited to the things you get a bill for. It is designed to be all-inclusive, taking into account all of the things, big and small, that you spend your money on. When you budget correctly, your budget includes even the things you have to estimate, like gas, food, toiletries, clothing, tithes and offering, prescriptions and so much more. Your monthly budget should accurately reflect what your real life looks like!

If you're realizing now that you've never done a real budget and need some help figuring out how to do it, I have included a wonderful resource to help you out. Once you have read through this book and are ready to start putting together your plan for success, jump to the back of the book where I have added the Beginner Budget Checklist. This checklist is going to walk you through step-by-step how to create a budget that actually looks like your real life.

Let me mention one more thing about budgeting before we move on.

In order to succeed financially, you will need to create a unique budget every month for the rest of your life. Yes, I know, you were dreading that news, but it is news that I could not move on without sharing.

The reason you have to create a new budget each month is tied to the simple fact that life changes and it changes often, which impacts what you need to spend money on. In February, you may be spending a lot of money on heating, winter clothes and snow tires, while June is all about summer camps, swim suits and family barbecues. In September, you're still buying last minutes school supplies and school clothes, but December is all about gifts, holiday parties and snowman decorations.

While you may not want to do a budget each month, you cannot deny that each month is going to be different from the last. It is for this reason that we need to create a unique budget every month to account for the ever-changing spending needs of our families.

PROTECT YOUR FAMILY

Before we get into the nitty gritty of turning dreams into reality, we need to protect the family from...well... life. Life is messy. Life changes fast. Life comes with natural disasters, emergency room visits and tire blowouts. The terrible truth is that if you aren't ready for life, it will take all of the hard work that you're about to do and flush it down the drain.

That's why you're going to hear me and every other financial expert tell you to make sure you have three basic forms of protection against life and all of the craziness that comes with it. You need an emergency fund, you need insurance and you need an estate plan.

EMERGENCY FUND

Your emergency fund is that fast cash that you're going to use when something in life goes wrong unexpectedly. This money is set aside for the sole purpose of covering those impossible to predict expenses that would have derailed your entire budget if you didn't have this stash available.

When our two year old burst into our bedroom with a 103 temperature, we used the emergency fund for the copay. When both cars started behaving strangely, we used the emergency fund to cover the repairs. When the air conditioning unit went out in the middle of June in our Texas home, we paid for the HVAC company with the emergency fund.

There are a million other examples that we can conjure up, but you get the point. When life hits you out of the blue with an expense that you couldn't have seen coming, your emergency fund is there to protect you.

Your emergency fund can be as big or as small as you want it to be, but the bigger the emergency fund, the bigger the emergencies that you're protected from. At a minimum, you should have $1,000 set aside in a savings or money market account for emergencies. I like to really recommend this amount for families that have debt eating away at their monthly income, which we'll talk more about later. Right now, I just want you to key in on that $1,000 number.

Why is $1,000 the minimum?

Take a moment and think about the last ten money emergencies that you have had. If you're like the rest of us, those emergencies probably included an unexpected car repair, an emergency room visit or maybe some random event with a child or family member. When you think about the numbers associated with those emergencies, at least nine of those ten emergencies were probably less than $1,000. Life usually hits us $200, $600 and $900 at a time, so if you have $1,000 safely tucked away for these moments, you will save yourself a lot of fear and headache a good 90% of the time.

Once you have had a chance to address those debts that I mentioned earlier, you're going to want to bump up that emergency fund to cover you for the big things, like a job loss. A good rule of thumb is to save three to six months of expenses. Having this much money in the bank means you don't have to panic if you're suddenly laid-off. You can spend the next three or more months looking for a new job that actually fits your family's needs instead of having to accept the first job that you can find for the sake of bringing in some income. Imagine how much easier it will be to focus on the interview when you're not freaking out on the inside about paying the rent or mortgage?

INSURANCE

Insurance is another form of protection that covers your family when life goes wrong unexpectedly.

It may seem like those monthly, semi-annual or annual premiums that you pay are going to waste, but the reality is that it is securing your protection from financial ruin when bad things happen. You see, insurance is one of those things that, like an emergency fund, can only protect you if you already have it in place. When you're setting it up or paying the premiums, it may feel like you're wasting a ton of money, but when life hits hard and you really need it, believe me when I say that it will truly pay off.

In its simplest terms, insurance is a transfer of financial risk. Typically, if something bad happens, like a medical emergency or car wreck, you have to cover 100% of the costs associated with it, even if that cost is far, far more than you can afford to handle. Insurance is the transfer of part or all of those costs to an insurance company, who agrees to pay for certain, covered incidents when things go wrong.

Imagine you're riding down the street in your car, minding your own business, maybe vibing to your favorite station on Pandora because that's just what you do when you're driving. You have to make a left turn and you approach the intersection just as your phone falls to the floor. On reflex, you reach down to grab it and BOOM---you've just slammed into a car crossing the intersection.

No one plans for things like this, but they do happen and they happen during random, innocuous moments that you aren't expecting. This is why having insurance in place is vital. After this crash, you would probably have to pay only your deductible of $500 or $1,000 if you had auto insurance. If you didn't, the bill is probably going to hit several thousands of dollars between car repairs and medical bills.

It is for this reason that insurance is vital to protecting your family. Paying a couple of hundred a month or year can save your family thousands of dollars when disaster strikes. I suggest five different types of insurance as part of your financial foundation:

- Automobile insurance
- Health insurance
- Homeowners or renters' insurance
- Long-term disability insurance
- Life Insurance

Automobile insurance covers that very type of situations that we just discovered. When car crashes happen, the insurance company pays the cost after you pay your deductible.

Health insurance is for preventative care and for those major medical emergencies. Many policies cover annual check-ups and age appropriate tests like prostate exams or mammograms after the age of 40. The policies also cover the big things, like emergency room visits and major medical events, such as a surgery or cancer. Thousands of families have had to shoulder the burden of cancers and other long-term conditions that can create over a million dollars in medical expenses. For most of us, a million dollars in medical bills would result in bankruptcy, and for too many families, it is a terrifying reality. The right medical insurance can prevent this.

Homeowners' or renters' insurance covers your stuff in case of loss or theft. Have a fire that burns your new house down, adequate homeowners' insurance will rebuild the house and the pay for all of the items that were inside of it. Or maybe you live in an apartment that was broken into. Renter's insurance will replace the stolen items.

Long-term disability insurance is intended to replace your income in case an accident leaves you unable to work. Maybe a random accident around the house leaves you unable to work from a year. After about 90 days, your long-term disability will kick in and help you pay your bills while your body heals or, if needed, permanently.

Life insurance protects your family in the event of your passing. If you leave this world, the last thing you want your family to have to deal with is bills you left behind and funeral expenses when all they want to do is mourn the fact that you are no longer in their lives. With the money received from the life insurance policy, your family can cover your funeral expenses, bills that you left behind and even cover upcoming bills while they pull themselves together or take on the additional expenses that come with caring for your children.

The truth is that insurance is complicated. When it comes to shopping for insurance, there are a lot of little things that you have to consider. For example, how much coverage do you need or how high should you make your deductible? Maybe you're wondering whether to add eye and dental coverage for your family. Ultimately, it comes down to researching the components of each insurance plan and determining whether those components reasonably reflect your family's lifestyle.

The best thing to do is to get the insurance that you need through your employer when you can. Big companies have so many employees that they can get massive discounts from insurance companies based purely on volume. Add in the extra perk of having the company pay part of your insurance premium, and you can easily get your medical, long-term disability and life insurance through your job. Through that same employer, you may even be entitled to some discounts on automobile, homeowners and/or renter's insurance with some of the major insurance companies.

The next best thing is to find a trustworthy insurance broker that is independent of the big insurance companies. An independent insurance broker that truly cares about their clients will ask questions to understand your life and family to help you figure out how much insurance is enough, then shop around your insurance needs to various companies to help you find the best deal. This helps you save money and who really wants to overpay for something that you may not need for years to come?

If for some reasons you're unable to get a good idea on how much insurance is best for your family, remember this: being over-insured can cause you to waste some money by paying more than you have to, but being under-insured can push you into bankruptcy by not covering enough of what you need. Do not be afraid to pay a little extra for the top-tier policy for a while until you can get a better understanding of what your family really needs. It may not seem like the best methodology in the short-term, but if something happens and you need that insurance, you will certainly thank me in the long-run.

ESTATE PLAN

Does your family know what to do if you fall into a coma? What about if you die?

If you have an estate plan, then they will.

Estate planning is essentially the process of planning in advance what's going to happen to everything you are responsible for (i.e. your estate) if you are incapacitated (think coma) or when you die. I say "everything you are responsible for" because this includes not just stuff like money, cars, debts and houses, but also your children, your pets and even your body.

Do you want to be kept on life support for two weeks or two decades? Do you want your children to go with your parents or your older sister? Would you like for a family heirloom to pass to a specific family member? Do you want a formal funeral or do you want the family to throw a big party celebrating your life? These decisions and more are covered during estate planning.

There are a couple of reasons why estate planning is so important.

When you have clearly stated what you want to happen, you minimize the fighting that happens between your family members. Imagine being in a coma and your children fighting over whether to do a risky surgery that will save your life, but probably leave you a vegetable, or let you pass on naturally. Or maybe your siblings are fighting about how to divide the 15 acres of land that you have after you left this world with no children. Or, even worse, the sister that does not get along with your kids is the one that takes them in, when you really wanted them with your brother.

This is the reality that thousands of families face every year because someone passed on without a Last Will and Testament or suffered a debilitating medical incident without a Directive to Physicians.

Instead of putting your family through this when they should be working through their grief, find a reputable attorney and have an estate plan created with all of your wishes. Yes, using an attorney can make this process a bit pricey, but think about the peace that you will give to your family by taking the time to do this right. Simply making sure that your kids end up in the right home should be enough to push you into action.

If necessary, create a savings fund specifically for estate planning. The best way to know how much to save is to first find a reputable attorney that handles estate planning and have a meeting with them. In that meeting, they will ask you some questions about your life and your family, and then provide you with information on your options based on what they've learned. Prices will vary depending on your life, because planning an estate for a single person with no kids is easier than for a blended family with four kids. So be prepared for those potential differences, but once you have a price, start saving the money as fast as you can so that you can get this vital basic in place.

UNDERSTAND THE RISK OF DEBT

The last thing we need to cover before we get to work is debt, or more importantly, the risk that comes with debt.

When you look at debt on the surface, it looks like a great concept. I get to receive and enjoy something now and pay for it later over an extended period of time. Who wouldn't want to experience the pleasure of that new dress or vacation today and worry about paying it off sometime in the future over the course of several months? It really does feel like you're winning.

The reality is that you have actually been conned. You have been had. You have been duped. And I can say that because I was conned, had and duped too.

The sad truth is that debt comes with a lot of risk that many of us simply fail to consider.

DESTRUCTION OF INCOME

The most obvious risk is the destruction of your income. When you commit yourself to making payments of $25, $125 or $425 a month for the next year or two, you have signed away that portion of your monthly income and you cannot get it back even when life changes on you.

When you made your commitment to pay this debt, you probably made some assumptions about your income. You assumed that you would still be in your job throughout the repayment period. You probably assumed that your income would continue to grow or that your expenses would stay roughly the same over the repayment period.

The problem is that life does not care about the assumptions that you made and your creditors certainly do not care when life goes awry. When life hands you a massive lay-off, you still owe that $425 car note and not paying it will result in some serious hits to your credit score before they come to repossess the car. If life throws a major curveball in the housing market, causing rents to shoot up $100 to $200 a month practically overnight (like it has around Dallas, Texas), the $125 that was going towards your personal loan may be what you need to keep a roof over your head.

Debt and your creditors do not care about the moments when life goes wrong and you no longer have the money to cover the debt. They only care about their money and if they have to make harassing calls to your home, destroy your credit, sue you, garnish your wages or send you into bankruptcy to get it, they will do it. Is that risk really worth taking when you could have just saved that money for a few months and bought what you wanted in cash?

But wait, there's more!

What happens when you have an opportunity to invest $500 in a business deal that's going to net you thousands in the future? Or what about that $300 class you want to take that could transform your relationships with family and friends? When you have to pay $600 a month on credit cards and loans, you think twice about whether to invest in that deal or take the class. Yes, they can transform your life for the better and you know it, but you simply cannot afford to participate because you have money tied up in something that you may not even have anymore.

THE INSTANT GRATIFICATION CYCLE

The risk that many of us overlook is the impact it has on our behavior. When you have the ability to get the pleasure now and not have to worry about paying for it until later, you initiate a vicious cycle that is really difficult to break. Some call it the Instant Gratification Cycle.

In the past, before credit was available to the average consumer, any purchases you made had to be in cash. This required you to save your money and buy it only when you could afford it. Gratification was delayed and we were okay with that expectation.

Now, credit cards and personal loans allow us to get the things that we want without waiting, creating an expectation that our gratification should be instant. We have conversations with ourselves wondering why we should wait to get something that we could easily receive today. The payments are small. The payments are no big deal. We have room in our monthly budgets to cover the extra expense.

With credit, we justify buying what we want now instead of saving for it and the more we do it, the easier it becomes. As we do it over and over again, we get to a place where delaying our gratification is nearly impossible, so we keep building more and more debt. This growing debt eats up more and more of our income and ultimately makes it impossible to create the lifestyle that we crave.

Is that really worth it?

THE CHANGE FORMULA

Now that we have laid the foundation for your financial life, it is time to understand how to effectively make a change, because you are about to make a very significant change in your life.

Please notice that I said *effectively*. When I say effectively, I mean a change that really sticks.

If you really think about it, we make changes all of the time. We change our diets. We change how we discipline our kids. We change how often we pray. We change how often we eat out. We change our hair color. We change when and how often we work out. We make tons of changes. In fact, New Year's Eve comes with a list of changes, many of which fall apart only a couple of weeks into January.

The real formula for making a change in our lives that sticks requires that we go through a three step process. Instinctively, we all know and understand these. The problem is that many of us will gloss over steps, do one out of order or simply not do one of them at all. Then we find ourselves struggling to keep making progress, slowing down bit by bit until we finally just stop.

Big companies go through this three step process when they make changes. They may break down the steps into smaller pieces with different labels, but ultimately, every logo change, every product launch, every culture change requires that they go through these three phases. And if a giant company with thousands of employees can get on one accord to make these changes happen, you can get yourself and your family on one accord to make them happen too.

What are those three phases?

First, you have to define success. Second, you make a plan. And finally, you implement the plan.

Now, to keep it simple, I'm just going to use three words: Dream - Plan - Do

CHAPTER 2 - DREAM

Let's cover step 1: Dream.

The concept of dreaming or defining success is to really understand what you want to accomplish and why. I can say all day that I want to get thinner, but what does thinner look like? Does it look like fitting into a pair of size 12 jeans or does it mean I need to fit into a size 4? And if it's about fitting into that size 4, is it so that I can feel better about myself or so that people will stop judging me about my weight?

Or you can tell everyone that you want to be rich, but how much money is rich to you? Is it an annual salary of $250,000 or a net worth of $1 million? Do you want to be rich so you can build a school for orphans or do you want to have money to leave to your children when you die?

WHAT YOU WANT TO ACCOMPLISH

Understanding what you want to accomplish gives you a destination to work towards, which is why you will hear every financial counselor, coach, advisor, expert or guru tell you that you need to set financial goals for yourself. The reality is that most of us are floundering with our money because we do not have anything to work towards.

Here is what we do when we fail to create our dream:

We will find ourselves in bed scrolling through Facebook and see an article with some money advice that catches our attention. We stop to read the article and by the time we reach the end, we are pumped and ready to go. We make commitments that about starting to invest, saving money, making millions flipping houses or whatever that article said we could do. Then about a couple of weeks into it, right around the time that we are starting to struggle to maintain the new plan, we are hit with another article with some different advice and the cycle begins anew. Next thing we know, we have done a little bit of everything and gotten absolutely nowhere! In fact, some of us may be a little worse off, because we were just doing stuff with no real destination in mind, which can even send us backwards financially.

To have any success in life, you have to have that dream to work towards.

Before we move on to the *Why*, it is important that I make one very important clarification. The dream that you are building is not a financial number. That dream is a lifestyle.

Remember that money is simply a tool, which means that money should never be our ultimate goal. The real goal, the real dream is the lifestyle that we want. Whether it includes traveling, a big house for the future grandchildren or quiet days spent on your family's boat, the lifestyle that you want to live is what you should be dreaming about.

It is from there that we can create our financial goals and it is those goals that tell us how we should be using our money.

Let's get started by envisioning the lifestyle that you want. I am going to push you into the distant future and tell you to dream about retirement. After all, you're eventually going to retire, so let's figure out what we want it to look like.

Close your eyes for a few minutes and dream about what you want to do when you stop working full-time. If you had 24 hours a day, 7 days a week to do whatever your heart desired, what would you do?

You've probably given it a passing thought, but I want you to build that vision until it's vivid. See the sights, hear the sounds, smell the smells, even begin feeling the things that you will touch. I call this building your dream in 4K Ultra HD! I want this dream to be so clear that you can smell the grass surrounding your country home or feel the warm beach sand between your wiggling toes.

Once you have your retirement dream, we can figure out what your finances need to look like for that to be a reality. How much money do you think you'll need between your savings and investment accounts? What about your home, or dare I say, homes? Maybe you have some businesses or a non-profit that you want to have in place. How big do those need to be?

For this step, there are tons of online resources that will help you estimate how much you need in retirement. If you have a retirement account already, the investment company probably has built-in tools to help you estimate what you need. If you don't, you can always check out one of my favorite tools, the Retire Inspired Quotient (R:IQ) at www.chrishogan360.com.

By the way, the steps you are beginning to follow can be found in the Resources section entitled Build Your Dream in 4K Ultra HD. If you want all of the questions together in a worksheet format, print or copy those pages and get to work!

One last thing. This exercise of dreaming about the lifestyle that you desire is not isolated only to your retirement years. If

THAT TOOL CALLED MONEY

you're a 22 year old who has just graduated from college, creating a vision for the lifestyle you desire at age 30, 35, or 40 is completely reasonable. If you just turned 35 and want to map out a vision for age 40, I can completely understand that too.

We look to retirement for two reasons. The first reason is that if you consider the life expectancy of the average person, you are probably going to retire, so it applies to pretty much everyone.

The second reason is that too many of us don't start to plan for retirement until we hit about 40. There seems to be something about that milestone birthday that makes you very aware of the prospect of retirement. I don't know if it's because you realize you've been in the workforce for nearly two decades or having people that used to mentor you begin to retire. Whatever the reason, around 40, retirement becomes something that you are acutely aware of.

And at 40, you also realize that if you had started saving for retirement back when you started working, you would be nearly 20 years further along. You think of all of the money that you would have in savings if you had followed the advice of those money experts and started saving just $100 a month back when you were twenty. You start to feel like you should be further along and you may even start to panic a little bit because you're worried that you'll never catch up.

If you're dealing with that sense of regret or panic, don't worry. It's not too late to build the dream life that you want. Just read the book, follow the plan and you will be surprised at what you can accomplish before you retire!

YOUR WHY

Another vital element of your dream is the *Why*. You have probably heard this before, but if you have not found yourself making progress financially, it is probably because you have not taken the time to really understand your why.

Why do you want to be rich? Why do you want to travel the world? Why do you want to leave your kids a million dollars when you die?

Your *Why* gives you motivation. Your *Why* keeps you moving forward each and every day, even when it seems like your dreams will never be reality. Your *Why* will help you handle temptation, ridicule, rejection and self-doubt. Your *Why* will give you hope on those tough days when you don't want to get out of bed or simply want to stop and give up.

Your *Why* is probably the most important part of your plan.

When it comes to my financial success, my *Why* is vividly clear. My *Why* is made up of the small humans that depends on me, the two younger brothers that look up to me and the God that created me. Everything I do in life, every decision that I make, and every sacrifice that I make somehow ties to one or all of those three. It is because I know how every financial decision is tied to my children, my brothers and my God that I can make them over and over again with confidence and without regret.

Understanding your *Why* has two elements, pleasure and pain, or as my mentor likes to call it: Heaven and Hell. Your Heaven is what makes this dream life so wonderful, while your Hell is the pain that you would experience if you failed to make it happen.

First, take a moment to think through the Heaven you and your family will experience once you reach these goals. How will you feel? Who would be proud of you? Would you be happier? Would you find life more enjoyable?

Then it's time for your Hell. What pain would you and your family experience if you failed? Who would be burdened by it? How much stress would you carry? What will your loved ones miss out on? What pains are you experiencing now that will not go away?

I have one more thing. If your Heaven does not have you feeling motivated, excited and ready to attack the plan, you may need to re-evaluate the lifestyle that you've decided on and the reasons behind them. A why that does not energize and inspire you is not going to keep you going during the tough days. That means you will eventually give up on your dream.

In order to do this right, you have to really dig deep and get really personal with yourself and, if you're married, your spouse. Does this dream really reflect your heart's desire? If not, take some time to explore what really does. This may take you a few minutes or it may require you to have a few hours of quiet time to reflect.

No matter what it takes, build a dream and a *Why* that truly reflects you or you and your spouse. Do not take another step until you do. It is truly that important.

CHAPTER 3 - PLAN

Now to tackle phase #2 – PLAN.

This one is pretty self-explanatory. Once I know what I want to accomplish, I need to know how I'm going to make it happen and, just as important, *When*! An effective plan has timelines, it has due dates, it has milestones that you can measure. This information is what allows you to craft your plan to get from where you are today to the lifestyle that you crave.

If your dream is to get thinner by losing 20 pounds so that you regain your pre-baby body, think about how different your plan will be based on the timeline you set. Are you going to lose the weight in three months or in three years? If you want to lose that weight in three months, your plan is going to be far more intense than the plan will be for three years from now.

Building a lifestyle is the same way.

Let's say that you are a 30 year old looking to retire at age 60. That plan is going to have a lot more wiggle room in it than a plan to retire at age 50. In fact, that ten year difference will not only increase how intense your plan is due to the loss of 10 years in the workforce, but it will also be more intense because you have essentially added 10 years to the amount of time you need to support yourself without a job. Changing your timeline changes your plan, so it is vital that you have one.

By now, you've probably asked yourself why the question of *When* was left out of the Dream phase. The Dream phase would seem like a logical place to put it, since you were mapping out your retirement and you probably know when you want to do it. However, deciding on the *When* during the

Dream phase puts you at risk of creating a timeline that is completely unrealistic.

Imagine that you want to pay off $25,000 in student loans within 12 months. It seems like a great idea until you realize that you only have $250 a month to put towards your debt. After 12 months have passed, you would have only paid off $3,000, leaving a $22,000 gap between your goal and what you actually accomplished. How demoralizing would that be?

This is exactly what we want to avoid. When you set a financial goal without knowing how much work your current finances are capable of doing, you risk setting yourself up for failure from the very beginning. Instead, we want to see how much your current income can accomplish and create a plan and timeline that takes this important reality into account.

So let's imagine that you're still looking at your $25,000 in student loans, but now, you're in the middle of creating your plan. You realize that you only have $250 a month to handle the debt and decide that paying off $3,000 a year is going to take way too long. After some time talking it through with a trusted friend, you decide to take on a second job that pays an additional $1,000 a month. With this additional job, you're now paying $15,000 a year towards that debt, which means it's going to be knocked out in less than two years with $5,000 to spare!

This scenario is exactly what we want for you! You created a plan with a timeline that matched what your income could handle and you even managed to bring in additional income to accelerate your results! By the time you're done paying off this debt, you will be primed and ready to attack the next goal with a vengeance!

This is how you build the lifestyle that you want.

Now that we know what this phase is all about, let's get to work!

UNDERSTANDING YOUR FINANCIAL PRESENT

Your dream lifestyle is calling your name and you've put on paper what your finances need to look like to make that dream happen. The next step to creating a plan that works is understanding where you are starting from. It's time to put your financial present on paper and for many, this is the first major obstacle to building a dream life.

Let me be completely transparent here. This step is scary! This step is going to fill you with a swirl of emotions that will have you pacing around the room, wringing your hands or even finding a place to lie down for a moment. Your emotions may bounce from anger to disappointment to regret to even discouragement. You will look at yourself in the mirror, questioning every decision that you have made and doubting whether you have the ability to pull yourself out of this financial pit without screwing it up further.

This is the step that makes people want to put their head in the sand and hope that everything will magically get better on its own.

The truth is that none of us want to be faced with our past mistakes, the results of bad decisions and the regret of opportunities lost. Just because we know that we haven't been taking the best care of our money and have dug ourselves into a financial hole does not mean that we want to look at real numbers and see it quantified in black and white. It's much easier to just pretend that the problem isn't that bad and that eventually, for some miraculous reason, the heavens will part and we will be blessed with financial success.

Sadly, that's not how it works

The only way to make forward progress with anything is to first admit and accept that we messed up, and then face the truth of our shortcomings. In the same way that an alcoholic cannot really rise above their addiction until they face the consequences of their drunken misdeeds; the shopaholic, the impulsive spender, the vacationing goddess, the king of eating out, the family of "I want it now" will never build the lifestyle that they desire without facing the numbers connected to their financial misdeeds.

So know that the feelings will come, but you have the power and the ability to rip off the band aid and face those feelings head-on. Once you have finally faced the reality of your financial present, you will be lightyears ahead of many of the people that are not living a lifestyle that matches their heart's desire.

BUILD A PROFILE OF YOUR NET WORTH

The first thing you need is a snapshot of your financial situation today and the best tool for that is your net worth. By measuring your net worth you get to see what would happen if you had to sell everything that you own to pay off your debts. Would you have money left over or, like many Americans, would you still be in a financial pit? This is a great snapshot of your overall financial health at that point in time.

To get your net worth, you simply subtract all of your liabilities from all of your assets.

$$\text{NET WORTH} = \text{ASSETS} - \text{LIABILITIES}$$

An asset is anything you own that, if you sold it, you could make some money on it. This includes houses, cars, retirement accounts, investments, jewelry, electronics, furniture, even clothes and decorations if you wanted to go that far. Most people stick to the big stuff, but literally, anything that can be sold for cash falls into the Assets column.

A liability is simply a debt you owe someone else. Whether it's the student loans, car notes, credit cards, bank loans, payday loans or even the $50 that you owe your mom, anything that you owe to someone else is considered a liability. Now, when we talk about liabilities, we're not talking about the light bill or the cable bill, unless you have a past due or unpaid balance. As long as you're current on your utilities, those should be excluded.

While many magazines and articles will use this as a measure of success, it really measures how well you have managed that balance between what you own and what you owe. Failing to balance this equation effectively is what causes families, even families that make millions of dollars a year, to file for bankruptcy.

When assets (what you own) are greater than liabilities (what you owe to others), you have a positive net worth and you're at least on the right path to making your dream lifestyle a reality.

If you own less than what you owe, then you have a negative net worth and you have some serious work to do if you want to build that dream life.

By looking at your net worth, you not only know where you are today, but you also have a really good gauge that you can use to measure your progress. As you pay off debt, you increase your net worth. As you save money, you increase your net worth. As you put money in smart investments that make you money, you increase your net worth.

It is for this reason that I not only recommend that you measure your net worth regularly, but I also recommend that you include a specific net worth as part of your financial goals. As your net worth continues to progress towards that goal you've set, you have a very clear idea of whether your plan is really working.

In order to help you complete this step without spending an insane amount of time, I have two suggestions:

1. For your liabilities, pull copies of your credit report from each of the three crediting reporting bureaus: Experian, Equifax and Transunion. This will account for all creditors that you owe who report their accounts to a credit bureau, which should be most of your debts.

2. For assets, limit your research to big ticket items such as homes, cars, boats, expensive jewelry, electronics or anything that you believe would net you over $100 on its own. For everything else, just use a low estimate. Many insurance companies will estimate the cost of your other personal belonging at around $10,000 to $20,000.

Once you have your net worth written down, it's time to move on to budgeting.

CREATE YOUR MONTHLY BUDGET

We talked about budgeting extensively in Chapter 2, so we are not going to spend a bunch of time here really talking about how to budget.

What I will tell you is why we want to build the budget now. When you check out The Beginner Budget Checklist, you will notice that it tells you to use your bank and credit card statements from the month before. The point of this initial budget is to understand what we have been spending money on. It is with this information that we can do the next step: Evaluate your discretionary income.

EVALUATE YOUR DISCRETIONARY INCOME

Depending on the source that you use, discretionary income is defined as "income remaining after deduction of taxes, other mandatory charges, and expenditures on necessary items." This is the income that people are always hoping to increase because it is the money left in your bank account after the bills are paid, food is on the table and clothes are on your body.

It is also the income that we are going to use to turn your dream lifestyle into your real life experience.

Take a look at your budget and complete the following equation:

DISCRETIONARY INCOME =
MONTHLY INCOME – FOUR WALLS – OBLIGATIONS + SAVINGS

What we have done is subtracted our basic survival needs and our obligations from our monthly income, then added back in the Savings category from the Obligations expenses. The reason we add our savings back into the discretionary income is because savings is one of our financial goals. Remember that emergency fund that you need? Your discretionary income is how you're going to create that savings, so it had to be added back to avoid double-counting your monthly savings amounts.

This equation tells you how much money you really have to work with to make your dreams a reality. When you're trying to save $10,000 to invest in a new business, you need to know whether you have enough to save $400 a month or $4,000 a month towards that goal. It makes a huge difference in your timeline!

This equation also helps you figure out whether you have an income problem. An income problem exists when the reasonable cost to survive and pay bills is more than your income can manage. Imagine how impossible it would be if you only had $100 left for the month after everything was paid. While it does allow for some progress, it can really be discouraging to see so little movement if we're comparing it to something like $75,000 in debt.

Notice that I said "reasonable cost" to survive. If the average rent for a two bedroom apartment in your area is $1,300 and you're spending $2,000 a month, the problem is obviously not your income. If your car note is $650 a month because you're driving a luxury vehicle, the problem is definitely not your income. So before you decide that you have an income problem, take a look at your expenses and do some research to see if they are in line with what others spend in your area.

When it comes to determining whether or not you have an income problem, consider the following guidelines:

- If it's going to take more than a year to save a $1,000 emergency fund, you have an income problem.

- If it's going to take more than 3 years to pay off all of your debt, excluding the mortgage, you have an income problem.

- If you have a family and less than $400 a month in discretionary income, you probably have an income problem.

I recognize that the last guideline can seem a little arbitrary, so let me walk you through a scenario. A couple lives with their daughter who is in middle school. The daughter participates in one extracurricular activity that causes the family to get home late multiple nights a week, so they often stop at fast food restaurants for $15 a visit 10 nights a month. The couple also believes having date night is part of a healthy marriage and spends $50 a month for their 2 dates. Already, the family has spent $200 of the $400 in discretionary funds, leaving $200 for savings or paying off debt, assuming the family does not spend any more money on anything else.

Tough, right?

If you discover that you have an income problem, increasing your income should be your number one priority. The reality of your situation is that you only have so much that you can cut out of your budget from an expense standpoint to make your dreams a reality. That only leaves you with bringing home more money.

If you don't have an income problem, you can still work on boosting income, but your fastest results will come from temporarily cutting your expenses in order to create more discretionary income. The most frustrating thing about increasing income is that it requires the participation of other people. With expenses, you simply make a decision not to buy something and you have accomplished what you need to. However, bringing in more money means someone has to decide to give you that money in exchange for a service or product that you provide. So you lose a bit of control over the process, slowing it down and requiring more work to get results.

So if you don't have an income problem, focus first on reducing expenses to increase discretionary income instantly, then move on to building your monthly income.

INCREASING YOUR DISCRETIONARY INCOME

In order to increase your discretionary income, you have to either increase your income or reduce your expenses. Yes, I know that you already figured that out, but I wouldn't be doing my job if I didn't at least write that down.

Now, there are thousands of resources out there with tips and tricks on how to make more money and how to spend less of it. As a result, I'm not going to dedicate a lot of time talking about every little thing that you can do. What I will do, however, is help you understand the general strategies that all of these tips and tricks were birthed from.

EXPENSE STRATEGIES

Let's start with expenses.

You have probably seen hundreds of articles and blog posts that talk about how to save money or how to spend less. When you really break down the essence of each of the methods suggested, they are really employing one of these three strategies.

1. **Eliminate some non-essential spending**

   This is where the oh so common but oh so controversial needs versus wants discussion comes into play. Everyone has at least one or two expenses that we treat as essential when they're really not. The problem with treating these expenses as necessities is we artificially cut our discretionary income, giving ourselves the impression that we don't have enough to make progress when we really do. All we have to do is sacrifice some things temporarily.

   A really common one is eating out at restaurants. It's almost never necessary, but you will see thousands of families on Sunday afternoon pile into their cars to eat at a restaurant when they leave church service. Or maybe it's the overpriced cable package that your husband says is necessary to allow to him to watch his favorite sports team play. Could it be trips to the salon that run you $200 a session when you really could have done your hair at home, albeit, less skillfully? What about that shoe or tie membership that sends new items every month for a flat fee, even after your closet is full to the brim with stuff.

To make this strategy work, you have to have a very honest conversation with yourself about what you really need and what you could live without. I'm certainly not suggesting that you cut out all of your wants, because I don't want you to be completely miserable and hate life. However, if you're trying to recover from some past financial missteps, you definitely want to consider cutting out some or, preferably, most of them.

2. **Buy items at discounted prices**
   This strategy has always been super popular and with the tools that you can find on your computer and on your smart phone, this strategy is just too easy to apply.

   Buy things on sale. When you're grocery shopping, you can literally plan your meals around what items are on sale. If beef is on sale this week, that's what's for dinner. If shoes are on sale, buy a couple of pair, even if you have to go up a size because you bought winter shoes in the summer for your growing child. Take advantage of the sales that you find to get the things that you need at a cheaper price. To make this easier, make sure you download a few sales apps, like RetailMeNot, Groupon or Ibotta.

   Buy non-perishable items in bulk when they're on sale. Whether you like to shop at a wholesale retailer store like Costco or Sam's, or if you like to hit the local grocery store, buying in bulk is a great way to save money. When you see items such as toilet paper, paper towels, or soap go on sale, buy up a bunch and stash it in a closet, the garage or pantry. This is a little tricky if you're limited on space, but I've see women in one bedroom apartments make it work, so don't think your small space makes it impossible.

What can also make this tricky is having enough money to make these big purchases. One way to save money for these kinds of purchases is to buy a gift card from your favorite store, like Target or Walmart. Every time you get paid, add a little more money to that gift card. Then, when a sale happens that you want to take advantage of happens, the money that you've built up for this purchase is already set aside and ready to use.

Learn couponing. Couponing has existed since newspapers and it has regained in popularity among women in the last few years. There are apps out there specifically designed to help you learn how to coupon and save tons of money. A couponing source that I have run across and downloaded for myself is Krazy Coupon Lady. Resources like this show you how to stack store sales with different types of coupons to get a lot of stuff for very little money. It can be a little time consuming, but based on the receipts that have come across my desk, the time is certainly worth it.

Buy generic. You many not believe this, but the store brand can really be just as good as the name brand. Most of the time, the extra money that we're paying is purely because of the name. So if the CVS painkiller works just as well as Tylenol, buy the CVS brand. If the Walmart brand panties fit just as well as Victoria Secrets, go with

Walmart. If the Target brand toilet paper is just as soft as Charmin, pay less by choosing the generic Target brand.

3. **Reduce how much you use of essential items**
   Let me be clear. I am not a big fan of this strategy, but it is a real and viable option, so we're going to talk about it.

   This method has a very simple premise: we would monitor our usage of our necessities so that we can identify ways to use less and reduce the bills and the shopping trips. While this strategy is certainly simple, it creates a strain on you, your family and your life in general. Think about the arguments that will come from monitoring your teenage daughter's water consumption. How many times are you willing to chastise the kids for leaving the TV and lights on when they go outside to play? Are you really interested in stretching the use of your body wash, your hair care products and your deodorant?

   It sounds extreme and it sounds miserable because it is! No one wants to monitor the usage of toilet paper and paper towels! I know that I don't! It is for this reason that I recommend you only use this method if you are experiencing a serious financial crisis. If you are being threatened with foreclosure or the repossession of your only mode of transportation to work, then by all means, use this method. If you simply want an additional $100 to pay off your debt faster, then I would say the strain on your life is simply not going to be worth the income you get to keep.

Also, make sure that you have a plan to make this strategy temporary. Essentially, you have to set a goal based on your financial crisis and then stop using this method once you hit that goal. Maybe it's once you fix the foreclosure or catch up on the car note. Maybe you need to last until the IRS wage garnishment is over, and then you can stop. Whatever the crisis was, stop using this method when it ends to regain that semblance of peace and balance that you had to sacrifice for that time period.

INCOME STRATEGIES

We've covered expenses, so now it's time to bump up your income. When you start talking about how to do this, typically you're going to run across five straight-forward options.

1. **Get a second job**

    First and foremost, this strategy is temporary. It is a band-aid. It is not your permanent solution because working two jobs can destroy your quality of life by keeping you away from your family and friends.

    When employing this strategy, establish a goal that you want to accomplish and then quit after you've hit it. Want to save $10,000 in your emergency fund? Do it and then quit. Want to knock a year off of your debt repayment plan? Work the second job until the debts are paid, then put in your notice.

    Lastly, when you're looking for that second job, do not accept just anything that comes your way. Take a moment to figure out how much extra money you need a month to accomplish your goals. Once you have that number, back into the minimum salary or hourly wage that you need to make on the second job so that it works for your family's financial needs.

2. **Get promoted at the current job**
    Getting a promotion is another viable way to increase your income, albeit, it's the option that you have the least control over. I recommend using this strategy when you really love the company and team that you're working with and hate the idea of leaving. If that sounds like you, use the following tips to help increase your chances:

    Demonstrate a strong work ethic. If you're not performing well in your current job, they're not going to trust you to perform well in a position with more responsibility. Show the "powers that be" that you are dependable, that you've mastered your position and that you are someone who people come to for help in your area because you get results.

    Find a mentor in a higher position. Finding a mentor will help you learn the things you didn't know you needed and improve upon the things you're already doing well. A good mentor can point out your blind spots, offer suggestions, applaud your successes, and guide your career. Think about who might be open to spending time with you to help you grow and maybe even spread some positive press by championing your skills, talents and abilities throughout the company to the right people.

Talk to your manager about your career goals, specifically goals that are attainable within your company. Sometimes we get overlooked because no one even knows that we want the promotion. Let them know that you would love the additional responsibility, that you would excel in that position and that the company would benefit from having you fill that role

Avoid the gossip and office politics. Becoming part of the office drama is a fast way to be labelled as unreliable, untrustworthy or just plain messy. No one wants to work with that or have that representing their company. So when the drama starts, do your absolute best to avoid taking sides, making comments or simply getting involved.

Dress for the position you want. It's all about showing them that you fit into that new role and can represent the position well. If supervisors wear slacks every day, start throwing on some slacks instead of jeans for work to show how serious you are. If senior managers go to meetings in a blazer, keep a blazer with you to wear when you're meeting with them. Consider it a bit of psychological warfare.

3. **Change employers**
   Changing employers is commonly used as a way to increase your salary doing pretty much the same job or as a way to get that promotion without waiting on your boss to decide to cooperate. The reason it works is that companies will typically pay an external recruit more

money than an internal transfer. It's crazy, but it's true. So it is not uncommon for people to move from employer to employer every few years, especially if they feel their career or salary at a company is growing stagnant.

In order to make this happen quickly, consider the following tips:

- Create a captivating LinkedIn profile to get recruiters calling you.

- Craft a compelling resume with action verbs and quantifiable results to grab the Human Resources representative's attention.

- Research companies that may have jobs similar to yours or have received rewards relevant to you such as "Best Places to Work for Mothers."

- Reach out to your network to see what positions are open or who they may know at a company you're interested in.

- Brush up on your interview skills so that you can impress your prospective employers once you land the interview.

4. **Change careers**
   Changing careers can get really complicated, be very lengthy and become expensive because many people do this by going back to school and getting a new degree or certification. That is really useful from a long-term standpoint, but it is not the only way to get into a new field.

The second way, which can be surprisingly lucrative, is finding a career that fits within your transferrable skills. A transferrable skill is simply a skill that you have to use to complete tasks in your current job that can be used in other ways at another job. For example, a person working in a clinic scheduling and admitting patients can use those same skills as a high-paid executive assistant for a group of busy corporate officers. Another person that supervises the operations of a food assembly line could use those same skills and insights to become a facilities inspector or auditor.

Transferrable skills are all about taking the skills you already have and figuring out how to apply them to a new situation. So as you look up jobs, don't doubt yourself if you haven't done that exact task before. Think instead about the skills you have that would allow you to get that task done. If you're confident that you can do the job, apply, interview and show them that you can.

5. **Start a business**

   With technology and social media, starting a side business and building it into a full-time career is easier than ever! You no longer need massive marketing budgets and big bank loans to get things started, especially if you're going to provide a service. Now, your audience and your future clients are at your fingertips.

   If creating a business on your own seems like something you want to do, consider this your quick-start guide.

1. **Decide what you want to do**: Do you have a passion? Is there something that's been on your heart to do? Do you have a hobby that you're ready to make money with? Have people been telling you that you should sell "that" – whatever that is? Then you have something with which to build a business.

2. **Know your WHY**: Take some time to dig into the why of your business. For example, a major part of why I do financial coaching instead of some other type of coaching is because I hate to see people struggle with money. All I really want to do is show them how to build a life that they can look back on and say "I lived well." When you know the why, it's easier to stay motivated through the tough times. So figure it out.

3. **Research, research, research**: In order to understand how to run your business, you have to do research. Processes, marketing, technology, pricing, when it comes to running a business, there is a lot to understand. If you want to build a lasting business that can help you reach you goals and maybe even replace your full-time job, do your research.

4. **Set goals (DREAM)**: What do you want to accomplish with your business? What do you want the business to look like? Creating a business is like any other change in your life. You need the dream of what you want it to look like and what you want to achieve.

5. **Build a plan (PLAN)**: Once you know where you're going, build your plan for how to get there. Leverage all of that research and build your business on paper.

6. Finally, **start your business (DO)**: The only way to start and grow your business is simply to do it. It doesn't matter if you doubt yourself, if you make mistakes or if you're a little, or even a lot, scared. Just do it, because if you don't, you'll never be able to succeed.

PUTTING YOUR DISCRETIONARY INCOME TO WORK

Now that we have a clear picture of how much discretionary income we have, it's time to put that money to work in building the lifestyle we've been dreaming about!

Just like with everything else, we're going to approach this systematically. We're going to approach things with an order with each action and each success compounding on top of the other. This is not a time when you want to start glossing over steps, changing steps around or completely skipping steps. You want to hit each of these in order and as we explain them to you, I'm going to tell you why.

Before we dig into those steps, I want to add to your list of life-long financial habits. The first habits on your list come from Chapter 1 and are to spend less than you make and to create a unique budget every month. These are the foundational things that you will always have to do if you want to build and sustain a lifestyle worth living.

The next habit is to stay away from debt by saving up cash for big purchases and events.

There are a couple of reasons why this habit is so important. The first reason is that you can never expect to get out of debt if you're always piling on more debt! Those credit card swipes may seem harmless at the time, but every time to put another $100, $300, $500 on that card, you're destroying $100, $300, $500 in progress that you had already made! That's guaranteed to become a frustrating merry-go-round that will slow down or even stop your progress altogether. So no adding debt when you're trying to get rid of it!

Second, who wants to do all of that hard work to get out of debt only to put themselves right back into the same mess. Have you ever successfully dieted, reaching your goal weight only to come back 6 months later, having regained it all? Some people do the same thing with their money. They focused on the short-term goal of destroying their debt than lost sight of the reason and got back in. Now they have to dig themselves back out of a hole that they were free from! Yes, you can get back out of the hole, but who wants to go through all of that pain and sacrifice again?

Save yourself the trouble and once you get out of debt, stay out!

In order to stay out of debt, we need to save in advance for the big things. Take part of your discretionary income and set it aside each month for the important things in your life. Do you have an important birthday coming up in 2 months? Start saving for it now. Do you like to do a big Christmas? Start setting aside Christmas shopping and party money in July so that you don't feel the need to pull out the credit card in December. If your car is entering into old age and you think it only has a year left to live, start saving money for a used car so that you're not coerced into getting a new car loan.

Some financial experts are going to tell you that the money needs to be saved in a money market account so that it can still make you some money while it's being saved up. You can certainly do that, in fact, I encourage you to, but ultimately, I don't care. What I really care about is helping you cultivate a "save now, pay cash later" mindset so that you do not fall back into that trap called debt and can focus on building that dream life we've been talking about!

BUILD YOUR FOUNDATION

The first thing we need to do with that discretionary income is to build our financial foundation. If you remember from Chapter 1, we talked about spending less than we make, learning to budget, protecting our families and understanding the risk of debt. It's the section about protecting our families that really requires us to put our discretionary income to work.

Here's what you need to do to build your foundation.
- ☐ Build an emergency fund of $1,000 or more
- ☐ Obtain all recommended insurances
    - ☐ Homeowners' or renters' insurance
    - ☐ Automobile insurance
    - ☐ Health/medical insurance
    - ☐ Long-term disability insurance
    - ☐ Life insurance
- ☐ Work with a reputable attorney to build an estate plan

Why are we doing this with our money first? Because the last thing we want to do is spend all of this time and effort growing our net worth, paying off debts, saving money, making smart investments only to have it all wiped out because of a single repair bill or accident. We certainly don't want to cause fighting in the family or put all of that hard work in the hands of the wrong person if we pass. Remember, the emergency fund, the insurance and the estate plan protect yourself, you family and your stuff when thing go wrong, and you probably know by now that at some point, things will go wrong.

So first things first, build your emergency fund of $1,000. Check out your insurance options at work and get in touch with some local, independent insurance brokers to help you shop around for the rest. Find a well-respected attorney with an honest reputation and build your estate plan.

Once you have the emergency fund completed, the insurances in place and the estate plan in progress, move on to the next step. Anything that you do with lawyers can take some time, so if it's going to take a month or two to get the estate plan completed, do not stop your progress to wait on it to finish. In this case, having the estate plan in progress is enough.

PAY OFF DEBT

Once we have our protections in place for the family, it's time to tackle the first big task: paying off debt.

In my mind, I can practically hear the groaning as you read this. Paying off debt is not fun, it is not sexy, and it forces you to once again come face to face with the reality of those financial decisions you made and now probably regret. I hear you! My husband and I went through the same thing when we were faced with the reality of how much debt we had amassed. It was certainly a very hard pill to swallow, but now, after having paid off tens of thousands of dollars in debt, we are living proof that you *CAN* do it and that you certainly *SHOULD*.

If that's not enough, go back to Chapter 1 where we helped you to Understand the Risk of Debt. When you think about how your debt is eating away at your monthly income, it seems like a no-brainer to get rid of those debts so that you can put the monthly payments back into your pocket! Imagine how much you could accomplish, the type of life that you could build if you were no longer paying that $600, that $1,100, that $2,000 a month to companies and could give it back to yourself!

To tackle this debt, we're going to employ what is commonly referred to as the debt snowball. The general premise is that you make minimum monthly payments on all of your debts except the debt with the smallest balance. This debt you attack with as much discretionary income as you can throw at it above and beyond the minimum monthly payment. Once you have knocked out that debt, move on to the second debt, taking the payments from the first debt with you to the next. You're going to do this over and over and over again until you have knocked out every debt on your list.

To get started, we're going to pull that list of liabilities from your net worth calculation. If you have any mortgages on the list, you can exclude those because we'll tackle those later. You're going to take these non-mortgage debts and put each one in order from the smallest balance to the largest. Then we're going to write next to each debt and each balance the amount of the minimum monthly payment.

It's going to look something like this:

Creditor / Debt	Balance	Min. Payment	Snowball Payment
Local Store Credit Card	$ 300	$ 25	$ 300
Personal Family Loan	$ 1,250	$ 95	$ 395
Car Note	$ 7,500	$ 425	$ 820
Big Bank Credit Card	$12,000	$ 115	$ 935
Student Loans	$ 15,300	$ 175	$ 1,110

Notice that we added a fourth column, called the Snowball Payment. This column shows how much you're actually going to be paying towards each debt when it has reached the top of the list. In this scenario, the family was able to find an additional $275 to throw at their smallest debt, the local store credit card. Once that card was paid off, that $300 they paid on the local store credit card was added to the personal family loan for a payment of $395 a month. After about three months, the personal family loan would be gone and the car note would be next. And down the line you would go

Simple, right?

Before we move on to the next step, let me answer a burning question that some people like to ask: Why aren't we attacking the debt with the highest interest rate first?

Let's go back to our example. More than likely, the two credit cards have the highest interest rates as the typical interest rate for a credit card is anywhere from 16% to more than 24%. The personal family loan, depending on how generous your family is, probably has no interest. So surely you want to hold off on the personal family loan and attack those credit cards first!

That may sound like a smart plan, but in reality, it overlooks one of the most important elements of your success: momentum.

For many families, the list of debts has a wide range, with some balances in the low hundreds and other balances in the thousands and tens of thousands. If you attack a debt with a high interest rate first that also has a high balance, you cause your momentum to grind down to a halt. In fact, if our imaginary family here paid off the Big Bank Credit Card as their second item, it would take 29 months! That's over 2 years working on a single debt! How demoralized and unmotivated would you be if you spent two years working on a single debt at the very beginning of your plan?

When you attack the smaller balances first, you get some quick wins under your belt fast that help you keep going! When using the debt snowball for our imaginary family, no one debt is going to take longer than 12 months to pay off. In fact, the first 3 debts on the list will be gone in the first 11 months of the debt snowball! If you could get three creditors off of your back in the first year of tackling the plan, wouldn't you do it?

I would! Frankly, I did! In our first year, my husband and I eliminated 7 debts from our list! Let's just say that it was a really exciting holiday season that year!

So follow the debt snowball. No fancy shenanigans or complicated algorithms. This is just a straight-forward plan to destroy one debt at a time faster and faster with each round.

UPGRADE YOUR EMERGENCY FUND

Once you hit this stage, congratulations, because you have made some mind-blowingly awesome strides! At this point, you will have accomplished something that most Americans could not even fathom: living a life without any monthly debt payments. This accomplishment is so epic, that I really want you to reward yourself. Throw a party, go on a vacation, do a little shopping! Just do them all with cash! Then you can move on to this next step of upgrading your emergency fund.

What we're doing here is adding more protection to your life and your family. Having $1,000 in your savings account is great, but it cannot protect you for very long from a catastrophic financial event, like a job loss or a high risk, experimental emergency medical treatment that is not fully covered by your health insurance. These are the type of situations that can put a debt-free family back into debt, so let's cover ourselves by building an emergency fund of 3 to 6 months of necessary expenses.

For most people, the question is usually how much is enough? We have a formula for that too.

$$NECESSARY\ EXPENSES =$$
$$FOUR\ WALLS + OBLIGATIONS - SAVINGS$$

At this point, since you have paid off all of your debt, your obligations number is going to be a lot smaller than it was when you used a variation of this equation to calculate your discretionary income back when you were trying to Understand Your Financial Present. This is super great because it limits how much money you need to keep on hand in order to protect yourself from a major financial event.

Once you have your necessary expenses, multiply it by the number of months you want to save and use that as your goal. Without any debt to eat up your income, you will be amazed at how quickly you can build up $10,000 to $15,000 in savings.

Then, when something bad does happen and believe me, it eventually will, you can rest easy knowing that your family is taken care of for the next few months while you work out a new plan.

BEGIN INVESTING FOR RETIREMENT

Now that you're debt free and you've protected your family from a lot of the financial chaos that comes with life, it's time to turn your attention to retirement.

Let me be very frank with you here. There are a ton of options out there for saving for retirement and unless you are a super investment geek, it's going to take you a lot of time and energy to understand them all and figure out which mix of options is best for you.

Since investing is not my area of expertise, I am not going to even attempt to tell you what to invest in and what not to invest in. What I will do is give you some rules of thumb to live by as you make your investing decisions.

1. **Invest at least 15% percent of your income towards retirement.** This percentage will change depending on who you talk to, ranging from 10% to 15% and sometimes even 20%. The closer that you are to retirement, the higher your percentage will likely need to be, but 15% is a

good starting point to creating a comfortable retirement, especially if you're still early in your career.

2. **Protect your money from taxes when you can.** No, I am not telling you to practice tax evasion or commit tax fraud, but I am telling you to take advantage of legal avenues to minimize the amount of money that the government will take out of your pocket when you retire. A popular method is to get a Roth IRA, which takes your after-tax income and invests it in a vehicle like a 401k. Since the money was taxed by the government before it was invested, your money grows tax-free. Once you retire and start receiving distributions, that money comes to you completely tax-free also.

3. **Have a diverse investment portfolio.** A big mistake that people make when investing is putting it all on one business, one stock, one mutual fund and hoping to hit it big. While this can work short-term, it does not protect you if something happens with that one business, company or fund and it loses its value. When the value goes down and never goes back up, you lose money. When you diversify your investments by investing in a lot of things, you spread out the risk across multiple businesses, stocks and mutual funds. That way, if one or two go down, the rest can keep growing or at least stop you from losing your life savings.

4. **Get a trustworthy investment professional that is willing to teach you.** These people dedicate their lives to making you money and can walk you through each of the suggestions that I've provided and more. The great thing about an investment professional is that the more money

your portfolio makes, the more money they get in commissions, so they have a vested interest in making sure your money grows. When selecting a professional, make sure that you thoroughly research whoever you work with and build a relationship with them.

5. **Do not invest in anything you do not understand.** Whether you have an investment professional or not, make sure that you clearly understand everything that your money is invested in. If your investment professional is not willing to walk your through what they're doing and teach you how they made certain decisions, fire them and find someone else. If some business person is trying to get you to invest in something, but cannot explain it in a way that you understand, walk away. You cannot afford to blindly go along with what someone tells you because, once again, this is *your* life savings we're talking about. So if you do not understand the investment don't do it!

ACHIEVE YOUR REMAINING FINANCIAL MILESTONES

Let's recap what you've accomplished once you've hit this stage.

- You've built a strong financial foundation that includes protecting your family from the chaos of life with insurance, an estate plan and an emergency fund of 3 to 6 months of expenses.

- You have eliminated all of your debt except maybe the mortgage.

- Your retirement nest egg is underway, leaving you feeling secure about your future.

Imagine how amazing, how powerful, how wonderful you are going to feel when this is your reality! If you haven't taken the time to celebrate your financial successes, you absolutely have to stop at this point to give yourself a massive pat on the back.

Throw a party! Go on a vacation! Check out a new experience! I don't care what you chose to do, but make sure that you do something to acknowledge the strides that you have made at this stage.

Once you are here, you have done a lot of great things, but you probably haven't seen that dream lifestyle come to fruition just yet. Maybe part of that dream is to have a paid off house. Or maybe you wanted to own a high-end RV so that you and your wife could travel the country together each summer. There may have been a charity that you dreamed of building or a series of small boutiques.

No matter what you had left in that dream, this is the stage when you start to make them happen!

If you have taken a peek at the Build Your Dream in 4k Ultra HD exercise, you have probably noticed the step entitled *Brainstorm the Milestones to Achieve the Dream*. In this step, you figure out the milestones that you need to hit in order to bridge the gap between where you are and where you want to be (i.e. your dream lifestyle). While many people tackle this part of the exercise at the beginning of their journey, this step is one that you're going to want to repeat over and over again.

Why? Because life changes!

When you first started this journey, you probably had little to no savings, a ton of debt and no clue how you were going to get it all done. Now that you're at this stage, everything that you do is different and the gap between your dream lifestyle and your present situation is very different. Even the current life that you're living could be different from children growing, career changes and even changes in geographic location.

So even if you did this at the beginning of this journey, stop right here and repeat the exercise. Take some time to right down all of the milestones you need to hit to make that dream a reality. Some of those milestones are going to be specific to the dream, such as saving $5,000 to start your first business. Other milestones will come naturally to life, such as saving cash for your daughter's college fund or creating a reserve to help your father when he goes into a nursing home.

At this point, don't worry about the timeline. This is just a big mental dump of what financial accomplishments you need to make for your dream life to become real.

Once you've completed your brainstorming session, you're probably going to have a long jumbled list of things to do. Now we need to put them in order and frame them with some timelines.

Remember that discretionary income equation? You're going to need that again, because once again you need to know what your income can handle as you work to achieve these milestones. You may need to save some money, but how quickly can you save what you need? You may need to make some smart investments, but how much can you afford to invest and how much do you need to get back?

When setting our timelines, I usually drop things into the following time categories:

- 12 months (1 year)
- 2 years
- 3 years
- 5 years
- 10 years
- 20 years
- 30 years

Notice that as I push further out into the future, the windows become bigger. That's because the further into the future you go, the murkier things become. You can pretty reasonable predict what your finances will look like 12 months or 2 years from now, but as life changes and evolves, it become a little harder because there is a lot more uncertainty. It is for that reason that I recommend that you really focus on the milestones that you need to hit in the next 5 years.

Once you have turned those milestones into goals with dates that you can measure, I recommend taking it a step further and breaking down the action steps for achieving those goals. After all, building a successful business is a lot more complicated than saving $10,000 in your saving account. Adjusting your career so that you can travel while making $100,000 annually is going to take a lot more strategy than the debt snowball.

At this stage, planning becomes really important, so do not slack. Do any research that you need to do. Start talking to people that have done what you're trying to do. Get mentors and coaches where you need to. Make sure that you gather as much information, insight and wisdom as you can so that you can make the individual elements of your dream lifestyle into a reality without it first becoming a nightmare!

LIVE A GREAT LIFE

You have done a lot of great work at this point. You're debt-free. Your retirement is set up and your family is protected from life's attacks on your money. You've hit financial goal after financial goal, celebrating each victory along the way. You will have had a really great life.

And then one day it hits you: you're living in your dream lifestyle.

It's a realization that will slam into you one day and you'll find yourself stopping to reflect on all that you've accomplished. Yeah, you've made some financial mistakes, but you dug yourself out of the hole you created and you've worked hard to craft a life that you and your family find great joy in. You're not stressing out about money. You're not staying up at night wondering what you are going to do if...

You are simply enjoying the great life that you have built.

At this point, I can give you all of this advice on what you should be doing with your dream lifestyle, but this is your dream, not mine. When you're no longer struggling, but living comfortably without the stress of money weighing you down, then my job is done and it is completely up to you to make the most of it.

So even though you, as you read this, are not at this stage yet, I do want to say one thing.

Congratulations Future You! You deserve it!

CHAPTER 4 - DO

The final step is DO, where you put the plan into motion. This step should be simple, but it gets really complicated because you're dealing with human behavior.

EXECUTION WITH CONSISTENCY

The first issue is that you have to execute every step of the plan with consistency. Have you ever struggled with consistency related to something? For me, I struggle with consistent exercise. I will train intensely for a while and then slowly fade until I completely fall off. I would much rather do my nerdy money stuff while munching on jelly beans than do 300 reps to keep my six pack, which is exactly why it is now gone.

If part of your plan is to take two to three hours each Sunday to meal prep so that you don't eat out for lunch and dinner; you have to be truly committed to it. If you have decided to increase your income by starting a business, there is going to have to be a lot of consistent, productive action on your part to make that business profitable. Or if you and your husband have agreed to drive to all family functions together to save on gas and wear and tear on the vehicles, there is some serious planning and commitment required to make that happen too.

The way that you overcome this obstacle is to learn what does and does not work for you to encourage the consistency that you need.

- Does having a friend, family member or coach holding you accountable help?

- Do you need to post a picture of your goals or your *Why* around your house, on your phone and in your car to stay motivated?

- Would getting engaged in a support group relevant to part of your plan, like your shopping addiction, help you?

- How about joining a Facebook group for part of your plan, like couponing or DIY projects?

- Could you create visual aids that track progress towards parts of your goals?

- Do you need to set small rewards for each milestone, such as a new purse when you pay off a credit card?

- How about establishing small punishments for missing milestones or making missteps, like doing 100 burpees every time you buy something on your credit card?

- Should you give your credit card to a trusted friend that you can trust to keep it away from you?

There are so many different ways that you can overcome the consistency obstacle, but the first approach that you try may not be the right one. Or you may need different approaches for different issues, like an accountability buddy for your shopping habit and joining a local networking group to build your new business. Regardless of how you have to do it, do not be afraid to adapt your strategy for staying consistent because consistency in execution of your plan is essential to your success.

LEARN FROM YOUR MISTAKES, BUT NO QUITTING

The second obstacle that people struggle to overcome is figuring out how to cope when they mess up the plan or fail to hit a goal. When things don't seem to be going right or when we feel like we're never going to learn to stay on track, our natural inclination is to give up. We convince ourselves that we've screwed up too many times to be able to fix it, or that we will never be smart enough, talented enough or whatever enough to live that lifestyle we're dreaming about.

Well, I'm here to tell you that that terrible thinking is false. You can make your plan work. You can build the lifestyle that you desire. And you certainly do not have to be perfect to do it!

Let's just get this out of the way now. You are a human. So that means you ARE going to mess up the plan, a lot. You ARE going to fail to hit some of your goals. You ARE going to backslide sometimes and do the very thing you knew better than to do. Messing up, failing and backsliding are all inevitable, but it does not mean that you quit.

Think about when you were a kid in school. How many times did you mess up an assignment? How many tests and quizzes did you fail? I certainly have my fair share of messed up assignments and failed tests, but somehow, in spite of those many mess-ups and failures, we managed to get our high school diploma or GED.

Mess-ups and failures are just a natural part of life.

What do you do when you give into temptation and swipe the credit card for that dress, or dip into your emergency fund to pay for a vacation that you really couldn't afford?

Recommit to the process and keep on moving.

There is no fancy formula or complicated trick. You simply have to decide that you are committed to the process of building the dream lifestyle for yourself and your family. Then, you keep taking one consistent action after the next to make it happen.

Quitting is a choice and if you want to live a life worth living, quitting is not an option. So don't let your mistakes derail you. Recommit to the process and keep on moving.

REVIEW YOUR PLAN AND ADJUST

The third obstacle in the *Do* stage is remembering to review your plan and adjust it when you have to.

We all know that the first plan you draft is not going to perfect. You may underestimate how much debt you really have or overestimate how many clients you're going to book your first month in business. Maybe you didn't realize just how much you were spending each month on your kids' extracurricular activities because the base month you used for your first budget was a slow month.

Perhaps life will simply change on you, which it does often and can do quickly. You may experience a small change in two months, like your kid joining the soccer team, or a major change next year after someone receives a dire diagnosis.

Whether there was a miscalculation in the plan or life just hit you with something new, you have to be willing to review your plan and make changes when necessary. Do you need to modify a timeline for one of your goals? Does your monthly debt snowball need to be reduced to accommodate a new change in the budget? Should you try attacking the credit card debt before the student loan because the interest rate is just that much higher?

In fact, I recommend that you evaluate your plan and the progress you're making at least once every three months as a life-long financial habit. Three months gives you plenty of time to work the plan and see positive results. So if you're at the three month mark and nothing seems to be moving, it's time to make changes to the plan.

Consider these questions when reviewing your plan:

- Am I on pace to hitting my financial goals?
  (Example: If you wanted to save $10,000 in 12 months, you should have $2,500 saved by the end of three months).

- If not, how far off the mark am I?

- What obstacles are slowing down my progress?

  o Did something change in my life?

  o Have I not made the changes in my behavior that I promised? Why?

- What can I do to speed up my progress?

  o What changes can I make?

  o Who can help me?

  o What strategies have I not tried yet?

- Do I have the potential to catch up and hit my goal on time? If not, when will I hit that goal?

Once you decide to make a change, make sure that you put it down on paper with the rest of the plan and start executing this modified plan with the same consistency you had before. Then, when you hit three months or life hits you with something new, repeat your review, update where needed and keep moving forward.

For the *Do* stage, this cycle of execute consistently, review, adjust, execute consistently will continue until you have achieved the very last goal in your plan. This, my friend, is how you create a lifestyle that you dream of.

CHAPTER 5 - NO MORE WAITING

Are you ready to take action?

At this point, you really have everything that you need to start building the life that you crave. You have a clear vision of your dream lifestyle and a *Why* that moves you so deeply that you can't allow yourself to quit. You have a plan that will lay down the financial foundation that you need to be successful and layer upon layer off strategy for making your dream a reality. You even understand how to be consistent, to review your plan and to make adjustments.

This is literally everything that you need to build your dream lifestyle.

It seems simple and straightforward because it is. It may not be fun. It may frustrate the heck out of you at times. It may even make you want to throw your hands up in defeat. But what it is not is complicated.

At this point, it is up to you to decide whether or not to take this plan and put it into action, but you may be sitting here experiencing some anxiety. Perhaps the simplicity of the plan has you feeling like something has been left out or is missing. Maybe you doubt your own ability to be consistent when you execute the plan. You could even doubt your ability to create the right plan for you, even though you have the tools and understand them. Or maybe, just maybe, you've been waiting all this time because you are so scared of failing or so convinced that you will fail that you can't bring yourself to make a move.

If you are struggling with any of those thoughts or feelings, listen to me and listen to me closely:

Understand that you are smart. You are capable. You DO have the ability to succeed with money. Say this to yourself and say it often.

Know that people who tell you that you are broke and will always be broke are suffering from small thinking. Even if the person telling you this is yourself, never allow those negative opinions to be your guide. Focus instead on the knowledge that thousands of people have become millionaires on small salaries by simply living below their means. You can too.

Remember that even when the progress you're making is slow, it's still forward progress and worth celebrating. After all, the tortoise won the race, not the hare. Your financial success is a life-long marathon, not an overnight sprint.

Finally, I believe in you. I wouldn't have taken the time to sit in this chair, backside going numb, if I didn't believe that you would succeed with this plan. The mere fact that you have made it to this paragraph means you are hungry for change and when you combine that hunger with a smart plan and consistent action, there are no limits.

No more waiting. It's time to use that tool called money to turn your dream into an everyday reality.

YOUR DREAM LIFESTYLE PLAN

☐ 1 - Build Your Dream
- ☐ Define your dream lifestyle
- ☐ Establish your why

☐ 2 - Understand Your Financial Present
- ☐ Build a profile of your net worth
- ☐ Create your monthly budget
- ☐ Evaluate your discretionary income

☐ 3 - Build Your Foundation
- ☐ $1,000 (or more) to start an Emergency Fund
- ☐ Insurance
  - ☐ Homeowners' or Renters' Insurance
  - ☐ Automobile Insurance
  - ☐ Health/Medical Insurance
  - ☐ Long-term Disability Insurance
  - ☐ Life Insurance
- ☐ Estate Plan

☐ 4 - Pay Off All Debt

☐ 5 - Upgrade Emergency Fund to 3-6 Months of Expenses

☐ 6 - Begin Investing for Retirement

☐ 7 - Save Money and/or Invest to Achieve Remaining Financial Milestones

Refer to the milestones from the Build Your Dream in 4K Ultra HD *exercise.*

☐ 8 - Live a Great Life

LIFE-LONG FINANCIAL HABITS

- Spend less than you make

- Create a unique budget every month

- Save cash for big purchases and holidays

- Stay away from debt except a mortgage

- Evaluate your financial plan and progress every three months

Your Step-by-Step Guide to Creating a Budget that
Matches Your Real Life

Getting Started

A budget is simply a plan that you create to tell your money where it is going to be spent that month. Your budget is one of your most powerful tools for achieving your financial goals, but for many people it seems impossible to do! This step-by-step guide will walk you through the simplest way to create a budget that actually reflects your lifestyle. Let's get started.

Tools for the Budget

- ☐ Last month's bank statements for each of your checking, savings and credit card accounts

- ☐ Last month's receipts, if you have them

- ☐ Pencil (trust us, you will have to make changes)

- ☐ Paper or a budget template

- ☐ Calculator

- ☐ Your spouse or Accountability Buddy

- ☐ **BONUS**: An app to put your budget into when you're done. We recommend EveryDollar.com, especially for beginners.

01 List your monthly net income

Net Income = The amount of money that you bring home after taxes, investment contributions, medical insurance and other deductions are taken out.

At the top of the page, list all of your forms of income:

- wages and salary,
- disability and social security,
- child support,
- alimony/spousal support,
- income from side businesses and odd jobs

Irregular Income = Any income that cannot be accurately predicted because it changes based on hours works, sales made, commissions earned, etc.

If you have irregular income:

1. Write down your income for each of the last three months.
2. Use the lowest income month for your budget.
3. When you're finished with your budget, create a list of additional things to do with income received above the amount in your budget. You may want to max out this list at the highest month's income.

02 List your "Four Walls" expenses

The **Four Walls** are the bare minimum expenses that must be paid so that your family can survive.

- housing and utilities
- groceries
- transportation
- basic clothing

If you have required childcare/daycare expenses so that you can go to work or life-saving healthcare expenses, consider either one as a fifth Wall.

List all of the expenses for each of these walls.

EXAMPLE: TRANSPORTATION
- car note
- car insurance
- gas
- oil changes/regular maintenance

03 Assign amounts to each of the "Four Walls" expenses

To get accurate amounts, go through your bank statements and receipts to see what you spent last month.

04 List your Obligation expenses

Obligation expenses relate to payments that are not necessary for survival, but are still high priority because they are tied to an obligation either to yourself, to your family or to others (creditors, religion, etc.). Examples include:

- savings
- tithes/charitable giving
- debt payments
- healthcare and insurance costs
- tuition and books

List all of the expenses for each of these categories.

05 Assign amounts to each of the Obligation expenses

To get accurate amounts, go through your bank statements and receipts to see what you spent last month.

06 List your "I Want" expenses

"I Want" expenses are exactly how they sound. They may feel like needs, but the reality is that you only make these purchases because you want to. Cutting these out of your budget may not be fun, but sometimes it's necessary. Examples include:

- sports and entertainment
- eating out
- kids' activities
- discretionary spending
- cable
- gym memberships

07 Assign amounts to each of the "I Want" expenses

To get accurate amounts, go through your bank statements and receipts to see what you spent last month.

08 Subtract total expenses from total income

This is the moment of truth, when you find out whether you have a surplus (more cash coming in than going out) or a deficit (more cash going out than coming in). If your budget comes exactly to zero, you are done and can skip the next Step! If not, let's continue to Step 9.

09 Make adjustments until your budget equals zero

If you have a deficit, start by removing or reducing expenses in the **I Want** group. If you have a surplus, find a place for the extra money. We recommend savings or debt payments.

REMEMBER: The purpose of a zero-based budget is to make sure that you effectively use every dollar coming into your home. A deficit leads to debt and unpaid bills, while any surplus typically disappears without a trace. Assign each dollar a job to do but assigning it to a category.

CONGRATULATIONS!

You have just finished your first budget that actually matches your life!

BUILD YOUR DREAM IN 4K ULTRA HD

CONGRATULATIONS! The fact that you're looking at this guide means you have come to understand how vital it is to have financial dreams and goals. If you have nothing to work towards, you will find yourself floundering. Either you feel as if you're financially stuck or you've realized that you're on a path that you never wanted.

LUCK FOR YOU, THAT ENDS TODAY! By the time you're done here, you will have a dream so vivid, you'll be able to feel the sand between your toes. And the best part is that you'll know exactly how to get there!

LET'S GET STARTED!

Build the Vision of Your Retirement Dream

Let's start by figuring out where we want to go. After all, eventually you are going to retire, so let's figure out what we want it to look like. Close your eyes for a few minutes and dream about what you want to do when you stop working full-time. See the sights, hear the sounds, smell the smells, even begin to feel the things that you will touch. Remember, we're building this dream in 4K Ultra HD!

Describe Your Finances in Your Retirement Dream

Retirement takes money, so let's think about what your finances need to look like to make your dream into a reality. How much money do you think you'll need? What about your home or dare I say, homes? Maybe you have some businesses or a non-profit that you want to have in place.

Understand Why by Describing Your Heaven

Understanding the "Why" of our dreams is a vital part of making them into an everyday reality. If you know why you're pursing that dream, you become more focused and more motivated. When you're working hard and sacrificing for something without knowing why you're making the sacrifice, you will quickly find yourself giving in to the temptation to stop.

One major motivation is the realization of some kind of pleasure, or simply put, to experience heaven. Take a moment to think about the pleasure you and your family will experience once you reach these goals. How will you feel? Who would be proud of you? Would you be happier? Would you find life more enjoyable?

Understand Why by Describing Your Hell

Not only do we need to understand the pleasure (Heaven) of reaching our goals, we need to understand the pain (Hell) of failure. After all, we humans usually try to avoid pain. So think now on what pain you would feel if you didn't succeed. Who would be burdened by it? How much stress would you carry? What will your loved ones miss out on? What pains are you experiencing now that wouldn't go away?

Put Your Financial Present on Paper

You have the dream, now let's look at the present and put it down on paper. How much money do you have in savings and investments? Do you have any assets like a home or businesses that are generating income? What about debts that are impacting your finances?

Brainstorm the Milestones to Achieve the Dream

You know where you dream of being and you know where you are today. Now we need to figure out how to bridge that gap before you hit retirement. Take some time to brainstorm every milestone that you need to hit in order to make that retirement dream into a reality. Don't worry about timelines - just write down every milestone that comes to mind.

P.S. Don't forget the random milestone that come with marriage and parenting!

EXAMPLES
- Pay of all $50,000 in debt (cars, student loans, etc.)
- Get children through college without co-signing student loans
- Purchase first rental property
- Obtain Master's degree in Business?

Turn Milestone into Goals with a Timeline

Now that you know what you need to accomplish, we need to give them a time limit. Take each milestone and assign it to one of the time periods below.

TIP: Do not overload the 12 month, 2 year and 3 year sections. Reference your budget so that you can figure out which milestones you can reasonably accomplish in those time periods!

---

12 MONTHS

---

2 YEARS

3 YEARS

5 YEARS

10 YEARS

20 YEARS

30 YEARS

Congratulations!

You have successfully documented what your retirement dream looks like in 4K Ultra HD. Even better, you also have financial goals that are specifically designed to help you reach the life that you want. Can you believe how quick and easy that was? If only everything in life was so simple!

Now the REAL work begins. It's time to start taking action so that those goals become reality and eventually that dream retirement is your everyday life! Allow these goals to guide every financial decision that you make, whether you are planning to buy another car, debating on your next career move or considering whether you really need another pair of shoes. When you have a clear vision of where you want to be, those everyday decisions that you have to make become so much simpler. So remember...

You Can Do This... I Believe in You

Tiana B. Clewis
Selah Financial Coaching

P.S. If you're feeling extra ambitious, we've included a bonus round on the next page! ENJOY!

From Goals to Action Plans

If you want to take this exercise a step further, you can take your 12 month goal and map out your action plan for getting those done. After all, saying you're going to pay off all of your debts in 12 months is a great goal to have, but you do have to actually do something to make that happen!

So how do we make that happen? By repeating this exercise for each 12 month goal.

You already have the goal and you've already written down your current financial reality, so you can just jump straight into the brainstorming step! In this case you would brainstorm every action that you need to take in order to make that goal into a reality. Check out this example:

GOAL: Pay off $30,000 in debt

ACTION STEPS:

- Calculate additional hours needed to make an extra $300 a month

- Make list of extra-curricular activities to keep and to cut

- Contact cable company to cancel cable (saves $120 a month)

- Have garage sale to raise money for debt payments

- Purchase used lawn mower to mow own lawn (saves $90 a month)

GOAL:

ACTION STEPS

Tiana B. Clewis is a personal financial coach and public speaker with Selah Financial Coaching, which she founded in 2016. Her professional career has always revolved around money and what people and companies do with it. She is a Certified Public Accountant, a Certified Internal Auditor and a Certified Fraud Examiner who has worked with companies ranging from multi-national firms to tiny family operations. She keeps her managerial and auditing skills sharp by serving as the Executive Director of Operations at her church home, Trinity Harvest Church.

Personally, Tiana is a wife to a pretty awesome guy, Boyd, who is also an entrepreneur and public speaker. Together they are the parents of four young children and one rambunctious canine. They reside happily in their home in Midlothian, Texas between trips traveling around the world to explore new cultures and enjoying the occasional adrenaline-inducing activity, such as sky diving, white water rafting and mountain biking.

ABOUT SELAH

At **Selah Financial Coaching**, our world is all about showing families how to make their dreams come true, and it just so happens that money is a great tool for doing that. With money comes the freedom of choice, but too many families are finding their choices stripped away because they just can't seem to afford the next big dream.

Learn how to take control of your finances and regain that freedom of choice with Selah. We will show you the money techniques that you need to create the lifestyle that you envision for your family. Managing money can seem tough, but we can help you make it simple.

Are you ready to take your first step to financial freedom? We're ready to walk with you!

CONTACT US

Thank you for reading *That Tool Called Money*. If you have any questions about what you have read or need more guidance on how to put this plan into action, feel free to contact us! We look forward to hearing from you!

CALL US AT **(817) 618-2069**

EMAIL US AT **TIANA@SELAHFC.COM**

TO LEARN MORE ABOUT SELAH,
GO TO **SELAHFC.COM**

.